Jesus, Above the Rim

A basketball journal about elevating your faith, hoops and family

D. Leb Tannenbaum

Xulon ELITE

Jesus, Above the Rim
A basketball journal about elevating your faith, hoops and family
by D. Leb Tannenbaum

Printed in the United States of America.

Edited by Xulon Press.

ISBN 9781498496278

www.xulonpress.com

God Bless You!

CONTENTS

INTRODUCTION

I have three passions in life: Jesus, basketball and family. This book is about sharing my passion with you. My intention is that as you read this book, you will identify and own your passion. This book really isn't about me; it's about you. It's about you and Jesus. It's about you and basketball. It's about you and your family.

Being passionate is a good thing. Being passionate and disciplined is a powerful combination. Being passionate, disciplined, and led by the Holy Spirit is the ultimate combination. It's the rare air of Jesus, above the rim!

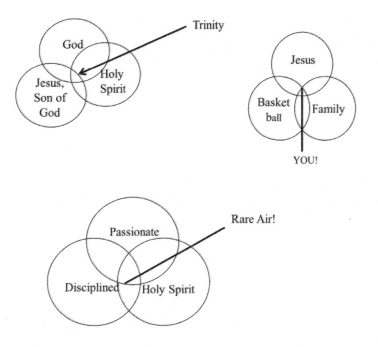

Before we continue, there is one other item we need to address. It's the question of faith. Should I be reading this book if I'm not a Christian? Should I continue to read if I am a Christian but don't know anything about the Holy Spirit? Should I be reading this book if I am a Christian, know about the Holy Spirit, but am so undisciplined that I don't even make it to church most Sundays? Or, should I be reading this book if I go to church because my parents take me and I don't choose to get much out of being there?

Whether you are a young man or young woman doesn't really matter, or if you are a parent or coach. Pay attention! The answer to all of the above is "Yes!" No further explanation is required, just a simple yes! Keep reading. This book is for you!

DEDICATION

This book is dedicated to every young boy and girl and young man and woman, to coaches at every level, to parents, and to legacy-leaving mentors like John Wooden and Billy Graham. And to all our brothers and sisters at the Fellowship of Christian Athletes (FCA) who recognize that success includes much more than winning games, and who value the rare air of passion, discipline, and the Holy Spirit!

ACKNOWLEDGMENTS

Thank you, Father God, for Your precious Son, Jesus, who always plays above the rim! Thank you for giving me a fantastic wife and seven amazing children. My quiver is full. Thank you to the leadership class that inspired me to get back on the court at forty years old. Thank you to my son, Abe, who asked me to coach his basketball team, which took me on a beautiful six-year run that included winning a city league championship. What a thrill! Thank you to my pastors at New Song Community Church in Portland, Oregon, especially Pastor Richard Probasco. You all rock my world!

PASSION

Let's talk about passion. When we talk about passion, we are talking about emotions. Strong emotions. Beat-your-chest emotions. Scream-out-loud emotions. Fists-in-the-air emotions. Quiet, fiery feelings too. You got it!

What comes to your mind when you hear the word *passion*? Probably all kinds of things come to mind. Some of us confuse passion with anger. Real passion might look like anger sometimes, but it is deeper than that. It is purposeful. It is positive. Listen to this:

"I like playing hard. I'll give 110 percent every time I go on the floor, and I'll do whatever it takes for my team to win."

    —Reggie Miller, the NBA Indian Pacer's "long-range bomber"

"One person with passion is better than forty people merely interested."

    —E.M. Forster

I love playing basketball with people who are passionate. Don't you? Give me four other passionate players to play with over ten merely interested players any day of the week. We may not have much of a bench, but we are going to play our hearts out!

So, what does passion in basketball look like?

Check out YouTube:

Christian Laettner: Duke game-winning shot

WNBA 2010, Game 2
Diana Taurasi: Best Women's Basketball Player Ever?

Seattle Storm vs. Phoenix Mercury: Sue Bird

Michael Jordan: The Last Shot! Last minute of the 1998 NBA Finals

Who comes to mind when you think of passion? Can you think of someone you admire who is a passionate person?

I can. His name is Jesus. Imagine this:

"When it was almost time for the Jewish Passover, Jesus went up to Jerusalem. In the temple courts he found men selling cattle, sheep and doves, and others sitting at tables exchanging money. So he made a whip out of cords, and drove all from the temple courts, both sheep and cattle; he scattered the coins of the money changers and overturned their tables. To those who sold doves he said, "Get these out of here! Stop turning my Father's house into a market!" (John 2:13–16).

Wow! To me, that's a picture of passion.

Now it's your turn. Let's see if you can share a picture of passion in someone else.

What does passion look like in your situation? Describe below.

_____

_____

_____

_____

_____

_____

_____

_____

Now, let's get personal. What does a picture of you look like when you're expressing passion? What age are you? What's the story? What did it mean to you? Another way to think about it is to ask yourself, "What was at stake?"

Here's my example: I was in my forties, and I'd been coaching a team of young men for five years. We lost every game we played the first year. We won four games out of sixteen the second year. In our fifth year, we were playing for the high school city league championship. At halftime we were up by two points. I started to offer some observations, and the team looked at each other, then looked at me and said, "Don't worry, Coach; we've got this one. We know what to do, and we're going to do it!" Everything we'd worked for was on the line. They were right! They were passionate! We won by twenty-five points, and it was a joyful outburst of passion when the last seconds ticked off the clock. I'll never forget that moment.

Now, let's look at *Webster's Dictionary*'s definition of *passion.*

Passion: "A suffering, especially that of Christ; any one of the emotions, as hate, grief, love, fear, joy, etc. Extreme, compelling emotion; intense emotional drive or excitement."

You just described a moment of passion. It may be easy to see ongoing passion in other people, but how about you? You just wrote about it from an earlier age in your life. Can you identify what you are most passionate about right now? Think of it as fire, a desire, or an interest that just doesn't die out. Can you see it? We are all passionate about something; we just express it differently.

It doesn't need to be complicated either. Heck, I'm passionate about eating good food! Write out what you are passionate about in your life now.

What I am passionate about is . . .

1.

2.

3.

"Love never fails. Character never quits. And with patience and persistence, dreams do come true."
> —"Pistol Pete" Maravich, a passionate basketball player

Exercise

Let's see if this can take you farther. If ten is a "raging wildfire" and one is "It's raining and I can't find the matches," what number between one and ten best describes your level of passion for the three things you wrote above? If you only wrote one, don't worry; it can take time to identify true passion.

Remember my three primary passions?

1. Jesus

2. Basketball

3. Family

I'd give my passion for Jesus an eight. I'm on fire for Jesus, but I know there is more before I can say I'm a raging wildfire.

I'd give basketball a seven. I love the game, but if I were fully passionate, I'd be putting in more work on my weak spots than I actually do. I can be more disciplined.

I'd give my family a ten. I'm on fire for my family, I pray for them all the time, we spend time together, we have fun together, and we enjoy each other and step in for each other if someone is hurting or needs help.

```
1-------------------------------5-------------------------------10
1 (can't find matches)      5 (a spark)      10 (raging fire)
```

DISCIPLINE

Now let's talk about discipline. *Discipline* is a tricky word. Most young people I talk to think of discipline as something bad. You know, "I did something I wasn't supposed to do, got caught, and now I'm going to get disciplined." That's one version of discipline. There is another version that is tied to excellence, not trouble. Let's look at this definition together.

Here is what *Webster's Dictionary* offers:

Discipline: "A branch of knowledge or learning. Training that develops self-control, character, or orderliness and efficiency. Acceptance of or submission to authority and control."

Basketball fans, coaches, and players frequently say that Michael Jordan was highly disciplined. His passion and discipline combined to create a powerful player, perhaps the best ever. Jordan was not perfect, however. The only perfect person I know of is Jesus.

Do you know any disciplined people? Who? How do you know they are disciplined?

Who _____

How _____

Food for thought:

"The fear of the LORD is the beginning of knowledge, but fools despise wisdom and discipline" (Proverbs 1:7).

"Discipline is the refining fire by which talent becomes ability."

—Coach Roy Williams, head coach of
University of North Carolina (365–108 career record,
eight Final Fours, and two national championships)

"Discipline helps you finish a job, and finishing is what separates excellent work from average work."

—Coach Pat Summitt, University of Tennessee,
Lady Vols (eight NCAA championships and 1,098 wins
in a career spanning 1974–2012)

Let's have you look at your discipline level with basketball. If the number ten is "Nothing can pull me off of my passion and purpose," and the number one is "I'll do it tomorrow," what number between one and ten best describes your level of discipline?

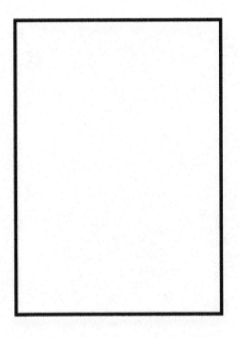

Here's another statement from the book of Proverbs to consider.

"Whoever loves discipline loves knowledge, but whoever hates correction is stupid" (Proverbs 12:1).

Now that's direct!

"It's all in the mind," says NBA great Reggie Miller. "That's what separates the good players from the great ones."

"I get up early to work out because it takes discipline."
—Chris Paul in his fourth year with the New Orleans Hornets, speaking about his 4:30 a.m. daily workouts

"I go to chapel before every game and I have a spiritual coach I talk to and he's helping me out a lot with my walk with the Lord."

—Kevin Durant, five-time All-Star, in a *Beliefnet* interview

Kevin Durant

Yes, the value of a disciplined mind!

Think about this. Do you brush your teeth, but don't floss? Do you work on conditioning, but eat food that's not good for you? Do you work on offense, but are less interested in defense? Can you keep your temper when you think the referee makes a really bad call? Do you intend to study, but get distracted by video games? Now look at the rating you gave yourself again and see if you think it is accurate or not.

Remember, passion with discipline is a powerful combination!

1_____|_____10

I'll do it   5   Nothing can pull me off
tomorrow.   my passion and purpose!

HOLY SPIRIT

Now let's look at the third element of Jesus above the rim, the Holy Spirit. First, we need to define the Holy Spirit.

Let's keep it simple. Here are a few things the Reverend Billy Graham has to say about the Holy Spirit: "We need to rely constantly on the Holy Spirit. We need to remember that Christ lives in us through the Holy Spirit. Our bodies are the dwelling place of the Third Person of the Trinity."

Wow! That means God's Spirit lives in me, in my body! Let that sink in. And with this recognition, that also means your body is important. That's why your foundation is important and your choices to keep your body clean and healthy matter in heaven as much as they matter here on earth!

Just to be certain, I went to the *Webster's Dictionary* again. First of all, *Holy Spirit* is in the dictionary. Interesting! Here's what is said:

Holy Spirit: "The spirit of God; specific, the third person of the Trinity."

The big question here is if you feel the urging of God's Spirit asking you to do something you might not normally do, like congratulate an opposing player who has been talking trash to you throughout an entire game, will you listen to God's urging and do it?

Consider this wisdom.

"Evildoers are trapped by their sinful talk, and so the innocent escape trouble. From the fruit of their lips people are filled with good things, and the work of their hands bring them reward" (Proverbs 12:13–14).

We will talk later about trash talking, paying close attention to what you say and do, and how the Holy Spirit can help you, especially when things get heated up.

Two things help me when I feel the Holy Spirit speaking to me:

1. Applying the discipline I'm developing, and being obedient to the Spirit.

2. Thinking of "the fruit of my lips." Is what I say sweet or bitter?

"Do not cast me from your presence or take your Holy Spirit from me" (Psalm 51:11).

Let's pause. We explored our passion, our discipline, and the Holy Spirit.

Let me offer a prayer here:

> Dear God, my heavenly Father, and Your precious Son, Jesus, please help me know and grow obedient to Your Holy Spirit. Help me hear that still, small voice in my heart, which speaks the truth and lights the fire of loving others when I don't want to, a love I can share with my coaches, team-mates, opponents, fans, and all people You bring into my world. In Jesus's name, amen!

If you've never prayed before and you just prayed this simple prayer, congratulations! Prayer is powerful. Our loving Father in heaven will help us and answer our prayers. It may take time, and it may not always fit our pictures, but He will respond.

There is another prayer to consider here too. If you have never accepted Jesus into your heart, you may want to now. The prayer is simple, and the impact is everlasting!

> Dear God, thank you for Your precious Son, Jesus, and Your Holy Spirit. Jesus, I invite You into my heart and believe You are the Son of God. I am Yours on and off the court! Amen.

THE COMPANY WE KEEP

If you are concerned that accepting Jesus into your heart will leave you lonely and not in good company, think again. Let's take a look together at some of the well-known NBA and WNBA players who openly proclaim their faith in Jesus.

Shanna Zolman—Indiana's Miss Basketball 2002 who played at the University of Tennessee under coach Pat Summit. She was the WNBA draft choice of the San Antonio Spurs, and ended her basketball career with the Tulsa Shock. She is an amazing woman of God.

Shanna said, "Jesus is the One who gives meaning and purpose to it all," and "He is who I am and the reason I exist."

Ruth Riley—Gold-medal winner and WNBA champion.

Ruth said, "I have confidence in my game because I know God loves me regardless of my circumstances."

Stephen Curry—NBA champion, NBA MVP 2015, and one of the best players ever.

After winning the 2015 MVP award, Steph said, "Each game is an opportunity to be on a great stage and be a witness for Christ. When I step on the floor, people should know who I represent, who I believe in."

Kevin Durant—In an ESPN interview, NBA All-Star Kevin Durant said, "Jesus Christ is Lord of my game."

A writer named Chad Bonham asked KD, "Are you encouraged to see a greater number of Christians—guys like Derek Fisher, John Salmons, Michael Redd, Kyle Korver, and Blake Griffin become more vocal about their faith?"

Durant replied, "It's unbelievable to know. It's good to see other people walk with the Lord too."

"I'm truly blessed to get up every morning and wake up and do what I love."
—**Chris Paul** in a YouTube video about his life.

Can you imagine playing with Shanna and Ruth? Stephen Curry, Chris Paul, and Kevin Durant?

Now let's give you examples of other men and women who have played in the rare air of Jesus, above the rim.

Ever heard of "The Admiral," **David Robinson**, NBA great with the San Antonio Spurs? He is a great example. Look him up! I'd build on the cornerstone of David Robinson any day. He is a mighty man of God.

So is **A. C. Green**, a former Los Angeles Laker. AC was known as "The Iron Man," and was a most excellent team member who earned five championship rings with the Los Angeles Lakers.

How about **Mike Penberthy**, who played for the Los Angeles Lakers in the 1980s? Look him up! He's a great basketball player and a true man of God.

Don't want to go back to the 1980s? Consider this lineup. **Chauncey Billups**, **Michael Redd**, **Allan Houston**, and ball-handling whiz of the Harlem Globetrotters, **Charles Smith**!

Prefer today's NBA All-Stars? Consider **Stephen Curry**, **Chris Paul**, **Dwyane Wade**, **Dwight Howard**, **Kevin Durant**, **C. J. McCollum**, **Chris Kaman**, and **Jeremy Lin**. These are all stated to be Christians when you search "Christian NBA Players" on Google. All are especially talented, and all are doing what it takes to be the best they can be, on and off the court. I'm sure there are many more not listed here.

In a 2015 *Charisma Magazine*, they wrote, "[Stephen] Curry is an openly committed Christian and the best player in basketball this year . . . . we do know that before he signed with Under Armour, he made it clear that he wanted to put Phil. 4:13 on the tongue of the sneaker with the underside reading, 'I can do all things.'"

The message is from Philippians 4:13, which states, "I can do all things through Christ who strengthens me" (NKJV). He may have turned down a more lucrative deal with Nike, but playing above the rim is not all about the money.

Dwyane Wade's jersey number is three, and it is reported that the number three stands for the Trinity (God, His Son, Jesus, and the Holy Spirit).

Jeremy Lin is an outspoken Christian NBA player. Remember Linsanity! Jeremy was wildly popular with the New York Knicks, and just completed a very good year with the Charlotte Hornets in 2016.

Many don't know that **Kevin Durant** attended a Christian school growing up. He carries a Bible in his backpack, and thanks God for his blessings as a star basketball player—even when he loses. At times, our faith gets tested. I'm sure it was really tough to be up 3–1 in the 2016 Western Conference Finals, lose three games in row to Golden State, and lose the Finals and a chance to play for a ring in the NBA Finals Championship. In an interview, Kevin put it this way: "I've got a long way to go to become closer to the Lord, but hopefully I can continue to stay on the path. I might take a few steps forward and take a couple of steps back and take some steps forward, but I want to get better."

Nate Robinson, NBA Slam Dunk winner, sent a message to Terrence Williams through Twitter, saying, "Just stay ready bro God will bless you, trust me. I play the way I do because God blessed me and I represent for those who get looked over." How cool is that! I always loved watching Nate play. His intensity and joy were contagious.

As we've seen with **Shanna** and **Ruth**, playing with Jesus above the rim isn't only a guy thing. Check out **Becky Hammon** in the WNBA. Becky has played for the San Antonio Silver Stars. Her stats speak for themselves, and her faith testimony on YouTube is awesome. Becky is a 2010 WNBA All-Star who was also inducted into the South Dakota High School Basketball Hall of Fame in 2010. A good year for Becky! She has even been featured in TV commercials.

Check out **Shanna "Sho" Crossley**, (married name of Shanna Zolman) a former guard for the Tulsa Shock, also played for the San Antonio Silver Stars. She played college ball at Tennessee. A three-point artist, she has too many stats and records to list here. The 2006 All-SEC First Team Selection and an *ESPN Magazine* First Team Academic All-American, Shanna Crossley ranks second all-time in Silver Stars history for three-point field goals made, third in Stars history for three-point field goal percentage, and is the only Silver Star to have appeared in every game over two consecutive seasons.

There are Christian coaches, college players, high school players, and many other NBA and WNBA players playing or coaching all over the world.

So, as you can see, you're in good company with Jesus above the rim! Let me mention one other, **Tamika Catchings**.

"Every Sunday when not on the road, Catchings found herself at church, alongside a growing number of teammates. At one point, six of the 11 players on the WNBA Indiana Fever's roster worshipped together at New Life Christian Center in Indianapolis, Catching's longtime church home. The teammates who built a spiritual sisterhood included Tammy Sutton-Brown, Sasha Goodlett, Shavonte Zellous, Erlana Larkins, and Karima Christmas" (Steven Lawson, "WNBA Star Tamika Catchings Offers Advice to Christian Super Bowl Players," *Charisma News*, February 2, 2013).

No big surprise that they won a championship together!

Tamika Catchings

"If God is for us, who can be against us?" (Romans 8:31).

FACING THE TRIALS AND TRIBULATIONS OF PLAYING BASKETBALL AND LOVING JESUS

Making the team is a preseason set of trials, tribulations, and self-discovery. Everyone knows from an early age that getting on a sports team can be both a great and a horrible experience. At the playground or school yard, if you are picked first, your reaction is usually, "Great, good choice." If you are picked last, the reaction is somewhere between, "This is humiliating" and "This sucks, and I need to avoid having this happen again." Well, those days may be over, but competing for a spot on a team can be a challenging experience. Having a good foundation will help you!

Foundations give you something to build on. Matthew 7:24–29 says, "Therefore everyone who hears these words of mine and puts them into practice is like a wise man who built his house on the rock. The rain came down, the streams rose, and the winds blew and beat against that house: yet it did not fall, because it had its foundation on the rock. But everyone who hears these words of mine and does not put them into practice is like a foolish man who built his house on sand. The rain came down, the streams rose, and the winds blew and beat against that house, and it fell with a great crash' When Jesus had finished saying these things, the crowds were amazed at his teaching, because he taught as one who had authority, and not as their teachers of the law."

We all know of some highly talented players who did not build their lives upon the Rock of Jesus and crashed. What you build your life on is important!

Exercise

Please take a moment and write down some of the things that have ruined the careers of some very talented players. If you're not sure, look on the Internet. There was a group of NBA players on the Portland Trail Blazers who behaved so badly they became known as the "Jail Blazers." Few of them lived up to their true potential. Make a list of the things that have interfered with the true potential of some very talented players whose foundation was weak.

1.

2.

3.

4.

5.

6.

You can see why their foundation crumbled, right?

Now let's examine some elements of standing on the Rock of Jesus together. These are often referred to as *cornerstones*. Cornerstones are critical for basketball and for life.

With basketball, ball handling, shooting, rebounding, passing, and defense are cornerstones.

Here are some cornerstones for life: purpose, patience, learning, listening, and speaking.

I will leave the basketball cornerstones in the able hands of good coaches everywhere around the world. All require discipline, passion, and the Holy Spirit for playing above the rim!

I want us to focus on the cornerstones for life.

Let's say another prayer:

Holy Spirit, please open my heart and mind to Your purpose for my life. Help me to hear that still, small voice within me that lights the fire of my passion and calms me when I need patience. Help me to realize there is always a higher purpose to reach for, and that Your plans for me are good. Please help me value discipline, open my ears to allow me to really listen, and guide my lips when I am speaking, especially when emotions are high! Thank you, Jesus. Amen!

Finding your **PASSION**—Let's look a little more deeply into what you are passionate about. You have the gut check, first look at what you wrote down earlier. I gave an example of Jesus chasing merchants out of the temple, His Father's house. There is a useful distinction I want you to consider. Let's look together at the distinction.

Interest vs. Passion

We are often interested in many things. We are usually only passionate about a few. In my life, I am interested in music, cooking, foreign languages, technology, art, and many other things. But my passion is for Jesus, basketball, and my family. They light my fire. It's where I spend most of my time. Let me offer one other clarification. God keeps expanding my understanding of who is in my family. Yes, I love and work hard for my wife, children, and grandchildren. I also have sponsored daughters in Columbia and Brazil with Compassion International. We've hosted girls from Ecuador, Germany, and Denmark who became like daughters. I have family in the church. God just keeps growing what I call family. Let God grow your family too.

Look back at the three passions you identified earlier. Do you need to make a change? Can you identify three things you are truly passionate about and place them in the cornerstone provided? If you have less than three, it's OK! More is OK too!

_____

_____

_____

_____

_____

_____

_____

_____

PATIENCE: "Able to remain calm and not become annoyed when waiting for a long time or when dealing with problems or difficult people; done in a careful way over a long period of time without hurrying."

Let me ask: Would you say you are a patient person? Would others agree? Let's admit it; we all get impatient at times. Prayer can be helpful here. I know that anyone who is rehabbing from a serious injury needs patience. Just read about Derrick Rose (knee), Kobe Bryant (Achilles tendon), or Tamika Catchings (ACL), or the years it took Greg Oden to get back onto an NBA court with the Miami Heat after a broken kneecap. The recovery process requires patience.

Some say recovery from injury is hard, but dealing with difficult people— that's really hard! Whatever the case, patience is precious, and is one of the gifts of the Spirit.

Consider these passages:

"The end of a matter is better than its beginning, and patience is better than pride" (Ecclesiastes 7:8).

"A person's wisdom yields patience; it is to one's glory to overlook an offense" (Proverbs 19:11).

"But the fruit of the Spirit is love, joy, peace, forbearance, kindness, goodness, faithfulness, gentleness and self-control" (Galatians 5:22).

Now let me ask you a *gigantic* question: Do you know why you are here? Do you know your purpose?

Here's Dictionary.com's definition:

Purpose: 1. "The reason for which something exists or is done, made, used, etc. 2. An intended desired result; end, aim, goal."

Answering the question about purpose is not something young people often think about. I didn't. If you ask me now, I'd say my life's purpose is directly tied to my three passions. I could say I exist:

1. To let people—especially young people—know that there is a living God who gave us His Son, Jesus, and that God loves us and wants a relationship with us that lasts forever.

"For God so loved the world, that he gave his one and only Son, that whoever believes in him shall not perish but have eternal life" (John 3:16).

"He loves. He gave. We believe. We live."

—Max Lucado, pastor and author

2. To share my love for playing, teaching, and coaching in basketball and business to create teamwork and flow that begins with a group of individuals who aren't a team yet and struggle to get things done together.

3. To offer the tremendous love I have for my family as the core for living unto God's commandment to "love my neighbor as myself."

"Jesus replied, "'Love the Lord your God with all your heart and with all your soul and with all your mind." This is the first and greatest commandment. And the second is like it: "Love your neighbor as yourself." All the Law and the Prophets stand on these two commandments'" (Matthew 22:37–40).

A person can spend their whole life living these two commandments!

I used to think my purpose was to be liked, to be popular, to look good, to get my way, and a host of other similar things. That's all good, but I now know that's not my purpose—neither is winning.

You see, I've met coaches who coach from a place they might call, "Win at any cost." If you've ever seen the movie *The Karate Kid*, you can see that's not the dojo to join. I'll stick with Mr. Miyagi or, best of all, Jesus! Check out UCLA coach John Wooden. He was one of the most-winning coaches in the history of college, but he was focused on a higher purpose of developing young men to be successful people, and he was a humble man of God.

Here's an illustration that may be helpful. We are talking about your "why."

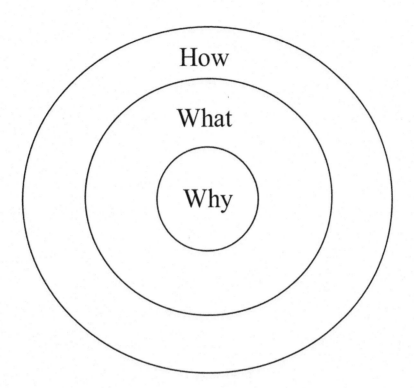

Most young people know their **how** (. . . do I become the best basketball player I can be?) and their **what** (. . . do I need to do?), but they often don't examine their **why** (i.e., what's my higher purpose for playing?).

Do you know why you are here? Take some time to write down what you think your purpose is.

Consider this:

"And we know that in all things God works for the good of those who love him, who have been called according to his purpose" (Romans 8:28).

"The one who plants and the one who waters have one purpose, and they will each be rewarded according to their own labor" (1 Corinthians 3:8).

Now let's talk about **listening**. Dictionary.com gives us this definition: "to give attention with the ear; to pay attention; heed; obey." As a coach, I asked my players to listen "as if their life depended on what was being said." It may not have been their life but it certainly effected their minutes played!

Here are some things said in the Bible about listening:

"Let the wise listen and add to their learning, and let the discerning get guidance" (Proverbs 1:5).

"It is better to heed the rebuke of a wise person than to listen to the song of fools" (Ecclesiastes 7:5).

"Then a cloud appeared and covered them, and a voice came from the cloud: 'This is my Son, whom I love. Listen to him!'" (Mark 9:7).

Here are some questions to ask yourself:

- When your coach is talking, are you listening?

- Do you tune in to things you like to hear, but tune out the things you don't want to hear?

- When your parents are asking you to do something or improve on something, do you listen as if you've heard it all before?

- If your teammate is asking you to pick up the pace or raise your energy level, do you welcome their feedback, or listen with "yeah, yeah" ears?

Really, listening is a lifelong journey well worth the investment. Yes, we need to sort out anything abusive or seriously negative. Constructive criticism, however, can be excellent if we can really hear it and respond!

Now let's look together at **speaking.**

Here is what the Merriam-Webster dictionary has to say about speaking:

Speak: "To say words in order to express your thoughts, feelings, opinions, etc. To say words to express yourself in a particular way."

Here are a couple of things the Bible says about speaking:

"One night the Lord spoke to Paul in a vision: 'Do not be afraid; keep on speaking, do not be silent'" (Acts 18:9).

"Instead, speaking the truth in love, we will grow to become in every respect the mature body of him who is the head, that is, Christ" (Ephesians 4:15).

After twenty-eight years of coaching sports and in business, I'd say the really successful players and people I meet have one thing in common: they are good listeners!

Listening and speaking play together just like point guards and forwards or centers.

Too much attention is paid to those who can speak well. I don't care if you can deliver a speech that ignites a fire, but as a coach, I do certainly care if you, one of my players, listen. Listening is a gift we offer to our coaches, our parents, our team members, our sisters and brothers, our grandparents, and those in authority.

If we listen well with others, it will help us listen to God's urging through the Holy Spirit. I actually have developed a passion for listening. It started as a discipline and turned into a passion. When I include the

Holy Spirit, it allows me to work the rare air of Jesus above the rim. Passion, discipline, and the Holy Spirit!

Speaking up can be hard for some of us. Some of us are introverts. Introverts are often described as shy, quiet, or private people. Some of us are extroverts who "talk to think." Extroverts like to talk and interact, and they get energy from communicating. There will be times in basketball and life when you have to communicate. Many of America's presidents have been introverts. You can learn to speak up and speak to a crowd even if you are introverted. Again, the Holy Spirit can help you discover what to say. God gave us a mouth for good reason. He also gave us ears for good reason. One mouth. Two ears. Think about that!

Let's assume your cornerstones are either forming or already in place. Then lean on the cornerstone of listening, because what we will address next is very important—life-and-death important.

THE BLOCK

Have you ever watched ESPN? Better yet, go to YouTube and look up the best blocks. People get put on posters because of monster blocks and dunks. Well, there are many ways we can get blocked from living our basketball dreams, and we need to deal with that now.

The question is how you deal with it. Don't let others' opinions block your passion and purpose. We all deal with what I'll call "limiting interpretations." There are also "empowering interpretations." Let's work out some with limiting versus empowering interpretations.

The first block is *you*! What are the limiting things you say to yourself, the limitations you place on yourself?

Mine was based on what I observed about size. After being a gym rat and totally loving playing basketball as often as possible, I looked around at my friends as we were finishing middle school. They were all 5-feet-5 to six feet tall, and I had just reached the lofty height of 4-feet-11. I told myself I was just too small to keep playing the sport I loved. That's a limiting interpretation! What limits are you placing on yourself?

Remember, the devil is a liar. He can even twist you into lying to yourself! He's like that worst fan, the loud-mouthed heckler in the stands screaming, "You're going to miss these free throws!"

Remember the cornerstone of listening? Who you are going to listen to is the key here. Imagine if Muggsy Bogues told himself what I said to myself. We would all have missed out on one of the NBA's most spectacular Slam Dunk Contest winners! Muggsy is 5-feet-3. Check out his YouTube messages titled, "Height Is No Obstacle" and "Muggsy Bogues Highlights." Then check out the Spud Webb Dunk Contest. Spud is 5-feet-7 and won the NBA Dunk Contest! Nate Robinson isn't very tall either. They didn't let their height stop their dreams!

"Confidence comes from practice."
> —Chris Paul, All-Star point guard with the LA Clippers

Exercise

Write out some of the limiting interpretations you place on yourself.

_____

_____

_____

_____

_____

_____

_____

_____

The second block is *others*. What are the limiting things other people place on you? What are others telling you that you cannot do well?

I walked into my first day of high school and the wrestling coach came right up to me and said, "You can forget about playing basketball; you're too small. Don't even bother to try out. You come and join the wrestling team."

I spent my high school years doing something I absolutely did not enjoy: wrestling! What I should have said is, "Thanks, Coach; I appreciate your point of view, but I have no desire to wrestle. I can always play basketball in a league in town if I can't make the freshman team."

Some common blocks from others are, "You're too stupid," "You're too lazy," "You're a loser," "You're too small," "You're too fat," and even worse, "You'll never amount to anything." Scripture says God loves me. He will never leave me or forsake me. I can do all things through Christ, who loves me. He will complete the good work He has begun in me! You get to choose who and what you listen to. I suggest you choose to listen to Scripture every time!

Exercise

I like to think of favorite scriptures as "words of life." Locate the "words of life" in the Bible that speak most to you! One of mine is Matthew 19:26: "Jesus looked at them and said, 'With man this is impossible, but with God all things are possible.'" Another is, "'For I know the plans I have for you,' declares the Lord, 'plans to prosper you and not to harm you, plans to give you hope and a future'" (Jeremiah 29:11).

I love that!

The third block is circumstances, coming back after you've been stuffed. My question here is how do you deal with failure? Do you lose your passion and "pull out" because you missed the shot that could have won the game? Do you give up on what you love because people who are important to you don't share your passion and purpose and say so? When things get tough, does the tough stuff block your passion and commitment?

Take a moment and write out your circumstances. Write down what you'd say are the good things, the pros. Then write out what you'd say are the bad things, the cons.

PROS   **CONS**

_____

_____

_____

_____

_____

_____

_____

_____

If life throws you a nasty curveball, staying focused on your passion and purpose with discipline can be difficult. Standing on the Rock of Jesus can straighten you out, even if your world is shaken with chaos. Unfortunately, some parents get divorced. Good people die. Maybe your dad suddenly lost his job. Maybe you don't even have a dad. Maybe your mom's health is failing. If you're playing with Jesus above the rim, you can deal with the circumstances and avoid the block.

"Come to me, all who are weary and burdened, and I will give you rest" (Matthew 11:28).

"Peace I leave with you; my peace I give to you. Not as the world gives do I give to you. Let not your hearts be troubled, neither let them be afraid" (John 14:27, ESV).

Now let's look at another thing in basketball that is always exciting and can be just as exciting in your life.

A clean steal: reclaiming what has been taken away (by yourself, by others, or by circumstances).

I was leading a group of people in business through the exercise we are about to do. I had just turned forty years old, and hadn't played basketball since I was fifteen years old. As I was taking the group through the exercise, it hit me like a bolt of lightning that this exercise applied to me too! A few people in the group saw the look on my face and asked, "What just happened to you?" I told them the truth. I had just recognized that I had given up on something I loved that I could still do if I would dismiss the old set of interpretations and circumstances, draft a new interpretation, and get back into something I loved! I'll tell you more later, but let me say now that I've been playing basketball again for the past twenty-seven years, and I don't intend to stop! I don't want you to lose years of passionate, purposeful living!

Reclaiming and dismissing limitations can be scary. Here's a favorite verse of mine that helps me: "For the Spirit God gave us does not make us timid, but gives us power, love and self-discipline" (2 Timothy 1:7). Power, love, and self-discipline; I want that spirit!

Here's the drill: go through your blocks. Some are limiting interpretations you've made or that others have said to you. The circumstances may be tough, but the way you think about them may be limiting. When you have listed a few, you are then going to rewrite them as empowering interpretations. Here a few of my examples:

Limiting: I'm too short to keep playing this game I love.
Empowering: I can do anything I am passionate about!

Limiting: Someone else (the wrestling coach) knows what's best for me.
Empowering: The coach has a right to his opinion, but wrestling is not something I will love, and I can say no to others respectfully.

Limiting: I am too broke to equip myself to play the sport I love.
Empowering: If I ask for the support I need to do what I love, God will provide someone to step up to help me or show me how I can help myself.

Exercise

Take your own limiting interpretations from the section you placed them in, and write out an empowering interpretation you can work from. When you are done, get above the rim and ask Jesus in prayer to release the Holy Spirit in you to lift you above your limitations and above your circumstances. Get prepared for freedom like never before!

Limiting:

Empowering:

Limiting:

Empowering:

Limiting:

Empowering:

Since you've been writing and rewriting limiting to empowering interpretations, now I ask you to write out a prayer. Write whatever is in your heart, and take this opportunity to speak to God in prayer.

Dear Jesus,

_____

_____

_____

_____

_____

_____

_____

_____

In Jesus's name, amen.

Don't know how to pray or what to say? Here's what Jesus said:

And when you pray, do not use vain repetitions as the heathen do. For they think that they will be heard for their many words. Therefore do not be like them. For your Father knows the things you have need of before you ask Him. In this manner, therefore, pray:

Our Father in heaven,
Hallowed be Your name.
Your Kingdom come.
Your Will be done
On earth as it is in heaven.
Give us this day our daily bread.

And forgive us our debts,

As we forgive our debtors.

And do not lead us into temptation,

But deliver us from the evil one.

For Yours is the kingdom and the power and the glory for-

ever. Amen.

(Matthew 6:9–13, NKJV)

Now add whatever you want to say or ask of God. I recommend you close with, "In Jesus's name, amen."

TIME OUT

Let's assume that you've made the team. We will also assume that you are past your initial blocks. Now we start finding out if we will play much or not. Before we address this, it's good to celebrate making the team! It's also good to pause, give thanks, reflect on what's happened, and prepare for what's about to happen.

Write out three things that you are grateful for:

1.

2.

3.

Before we get into playing time, let me ask you a question. What is the purpose of time out? List some of the reasons a coach will call, "Time out!" in practice or a competitive basketball game. See if you can get to a list of five reasons why.

1.

2.

3.

4.

5.

Time outs are important to the game, and are just as important to you.

It's unfortunate that teachers and parents have often spoiled the valuable sense of calling a time out by using them mostly to discipline for bad or unwanted behavior. This hooks up "You're bad," with "Go take a time out." So, to be a little different, let's call it a "time out of time."

Time out of time is when you pull yourself "out," giving yourself a little time to think, to look, to listen, and to pray.

Jesus went off by himself to pray, to be with His Father, to listen to that still small voice inside of us (John 6:15).

Time out of time's are valuable. Take one when you need one. Here are some useful questions you might ask when you're in time out of time (TOOT):

- What just happened?

- What's going on with them?

- What's going on with me?

- What in these circumstances can I control? What can't I control?

- What am I feeling about this? Why?

- If I was the coach, what would I say is working well? Not well? What needs to change?

- Who can I talk to about this?

- How are my teammates doing?

- Who should I be praying for?

- What is the Holy Spirit telling me?

Taking a personal time out may actually determine how your coach and teammates see you and impact the number of minutes you are chosen to play each game. It is important to always be prepared and to be of a sound mind.

When I was a coach, here are a few reasons I called a time out in a game:

1. We are not following our game plan, and we are playing into their plan.

2. We are getting out-hustled.

3. We are playing great, and our players look like they could use a break.

4. It's getting too intense out there with the opposing team and/or referees.

5. The momentum has changed against us, and the home crowd is feeding their energy.

6. I want the players on the court to huddle, to say what they are seeing, and to figure out what to do about it.

7. I want to call for a specific play to be executed.

LISTEN! (But not to everything.)

The Bible points out that the sheep know the voice of the Shepard. Jesus talks about this. The sheep trust the Shepard because He cares for them. He will fight for them. He will go find the one who is lost. He will even give His own life for them.

How many of you can tell when you are hearing the urges of God as opposed to the voices of all those around you? It's not always easy to know, but it is possible.

If God or the Holy Spirit is speaking, listening is the most important thing you can do. Let me tell you another short story. I was facilitating a business meeting. For two hours, I sat and listened to the vice president of sales lay out the plan for the next year. His whole sales team was there, and they had just come back from a large trade show where they had met with most of their key customers. For about an hour, God kept trying to make me see something that made my stomach tighten and my discomfort grow. Then, suddenly, I heard this audible whisper in my soul, and a question was formed. I thought my consulting buddy had leaned over and whispered in my ear. He hadn't.

"Ask them what we aren't talking about."

My first response was, "What?" It was followed by, "Lord, I can't just do that." Then came the test of obedience. Would I say "Yes, Lord?"

So, I stopped the meeting and said, "I know what we have been talking about for the past two hours. What is it we're not talking about?"

It got so quiet you could hear a pin drop. The vice president of sales lay his forehead on the table and began to sob. I had no idea why. He said in the midst of tears and literal sobbing that he and the whole team had been doing some wildly inappropriate things at the trade show they had all just come back from. Right then and there, he confessed it all.

Lives were changed for the better out of asking that question. I had heard from God and submitted to His will, and something I never would have dreamed of happened. This doesn't happen often. What I want you to know is that as your faith grows, God can call on us to use our lives for His good purposes. You have to listen. You have to submit. You have to be obedient.

It's almost the same with your coach. You have to submit to him or her. There is nothing more frustrating to a coach then young players who don't listen. Trust me. I've coached on and off for ten years. Coaches can't always get the refs to listen, but their own kids? They expect them to listen! That's why they will ask when they are instructing in practice, "What did I just say?" If you can't respond because you weren't really listening, a lot of push-ups usually follow. Rightfully so!

Let's remember: listening is a discipline. It is one of life's cornerstones. Listening is a lifelong learning. Great listeners advance in life. I hope you're listening!

Listening also requires a word that may be new to you, *discernment.* Dictionary.com defines discernment as "the ability to perceive by sight or some other sense or by the intellect; see, recognize, or apprehend." Respect your coach, but realize everything he or she has to offer may not be in your best interest. Remember this: God is the ultimate head coach, and Jesus, His Son, is above the rim. We are called to be a light in the world, but not to be of the world, not conforming to the world's view of basketball players.

Here's an example: When I left what I loved and joined my high school wrestling team, my coach constantly pressured me to lose weight. Rather than building me up, in reality, he was tearing me down to get someone who could wrestle in the lightest weights. His motive was selfish, and if I was listening to my heart, using godly discernment, and being wise (which isn't easy to do at fifteen years old!), I would have said no. I should have respectfully declined, hit the weight room, and made myself the best I could be at my natural weight.

I think of discernment like listening to a radio station that is fuzzy and just a little off. Listen closely and make that necessary adjustment, and suddenly the signal comes in loud and clear!

Exercise

Where do you need to exercise discernment right now in your life? Examples may be:

- Who and what do I listen to (including music!)?

- As a player, when do I need to speak up and when do I need to let my actions speak for themselves?

- Is there an area in my life that I'm confused by?

- How are my teammates doing?

- Do I have an important decision to make? Have I prayed about it?

- Have I asked for Godly discernment?

Write out a few notes here on what you may need discernment about:

_____

_____

_____

_____

_____

_____

_____

_____

Now let's talk about *winning*. Winning isn't everything. Being the *best you* is.

Exercise

Go online and look up all the number-one NBA Draft Picks for the past twenty years. How good were those picks? How many are remembered, and for what? Then, look up all the NCAA (college) basketball champions for the past twenty years. What are all of those players doing today? My point is that winning fades. Being the best you is a lifetime event. Think about it!

Exercise

Write a paragraph that describes the best you on and off the court. It might begin with, "Here's what me at my best looks like . . ." or "When I'm at my best, I . . ."

_____

_____

_____

_____

_____

_____

_____

_____

Exercise

Check out David Robinson, aka "The Admiral." Check out A. C. Green, aka "The Iron Man." Check out Stephen Curry, Kevin Durant, Chris Paul, C. J. McCollum, and a host of other NBA players. Look up Mike Penberthy (1980s). Search the WNBA. Check out Becky Hammon. Read about Shanna "Sho" Crossley and Tamika Catchings. What are they known for on the court? Better yet, what are they known for off the court? What are they doing now? Are they still playing above the rim? Are they doing something for others that makes God smile? Not every player gets to wear a championship ring, but every player who plays above the rim gets to be a difference maker on and off the court!

Winning requires trust in yourself and others. Trust is the foundation of relationships. Look at a dollar bill from the United States. It says on it, "In God we trust." Think of your best friend. Do you trust each other? Great teams are built on trust. Winning on the court requires trust. Winning off the court requires trust. Where do you place your trust? One of the wisest decisions you can make in life is to put your trust in Jesus.

If you haven't done this yet and you know you want to, let's take a TOOT (time out of time) and give you time to pray. It doesn't need to be complicated. It can be as simple as getting on your knees and saying, "Dear Jesus, Heavenly Father, I ask You into my heart. I give myself to You as my Lord and Savior. Thank you for loving me just the way I am. I believe in Your Word and know You will never leave me or forsake me, and that You will complete the good work You have started in me! Amen."

Very cool! Now remember, the Bible tells us that all His promises are true. This doesn't mean you will get everything you want. This doesn't mean you won't have to work hard to be the best you. It does mean He will do what He has promised. This is simply *awesome*! Keeping promises is powerful. I promise you, right now, if you become a promise keeper, you will stand out in all you do. Live this way and place your trust in Jesus, and you will soar above the rim!

Remember, keeping promises builds trust. Let me ask you this. What are you doing to build trust? What are you doing that limits or breaks trust? Think of it this way. Trust is currency, and promise keepers are rich!

IT'S GAME TIME!

Girls Basketball

You've practiced, you've work hard, you've given your best, and now the season begins. Whether you are starting, coming off the bench, or concerned you will never get off the bench, being ready is important.

There are many examples in the Bible illustrating God clearly calling someone's "number" and then showing their response and readiness.

Was Moses ready to accept God's call? Not at first!

Was Jonah ready and willing to do what God asked of him? No, and he found himself in the belly of a whale!

How about King David? The answer here is that sometimes he was and sometimes he wasn't. He made some tragic mistakes by choosing his own will and way before repenting and getting back into God's will.

Was Mary, the mother of Jesus, ready and willing? Her answer was beautifully simple. "'I am the Lord's servant,' Mary answered. 'May your word to me be fulfilled.' Then the angel left her" (Luke 1:38).

If the coach calls your name, are you ready? Always remaining ready is key to playing above the rim! If you are starting, being mentally, physically, and spiritually ready from tip-off to the final buzzer is what we're talking about.

There are many ways to be "ready." If you are coming off the bench, have you been just sitting on the bench, or have you been watching the game intensely, seeing what the offense and defense are doing and getting yourself prepared to step in?

What if your coach calls a play and says you're the one to take the shot? Are you ready? Do you know the coach's plays? Have you been practicing enough to be ready for this moment? There are many great players who come off the bench. Do you know that there is an award in the NBA titled the Sixth Man of the Year Award? This is a player who is usually first off the bench and contributes game after game in a big way! Check out Jamal Crawford of the LA Clippers. He won the Sixth Man of the Year Award in 2015, and then won it again in 2016! He doesn't start, but he doesn't mope about it. He contributes!

Now let's imagine you in the setting of a game.

FIRST QUARTER—FOLLOW THE PLAN

Just as God has a good plan for each one of us, every good coach has a game plan he or she is asking his or her team to follow.

God does this too. He essentially says in Jeremiah 29:11, "I have plans for you. Good plans. Plans to make you prosper."

One element of almost every first quarter plan is to rebound, rebound, and rebound. Set the tone and rebound. I like to think of rebounds as God's mercy and forgiveness. We make a mistake. We acknowledge it. We repent. God forgives.

We miss a shot. A teammate rebounds the miss. We reload. We score. They miss a shot. We don't let them reload. We rebound. Offensive rebounds. Defensive rebounds. God's forgiveness and redemption. In most cases, the team that grabs the most rebounds wins the game.

This may sound weird, but God uses the fools of this world for His great purposes.

"But God chose the foolish things of the world to shame the wise" (1 Corinthians 1:27).

So, be a rebounding fool! Anticipate. Jump. Fight for that loose ball. Coaches love a rebounding fool! Follow the coach's first-quarter game plan.

Wait! We're not done yet. What else happens when we rebound and follow the first-quarter game plan? Something exciting! It often goes something like this: "Defensive rebound! Outlet pass! Fast break! Score!!!"

Now I have your attention, right? Fast breaks are fun. They're flashy. They might lead to a dunk. The crowd goes wild! It's all good if it happens within the plan. And where does the fast break begin? It begins with a "That's mine!" rebound, or with active hands that deflect a pass. Defense creates offense. It's true in life too. If life is pressing in, if you've made a mistake in a game, rebuke those negative thoughts in Jesus's name. The rebuke is like a rebound! Repeat to yourself a favorite line of Scripture. Say a quick prayer in Jesus's name. Consider it answered and move on! Nobody but Jesus was perfect. We all do things that separate us from God. Each and every one of us falls short. We all make mistakes.

"There is no difference between Jew and Gentile, for all have sinned and fall short of the glory of God" (Romans 3:23).

We are also loved by God just the way we are. After all, He created us! "For God so loved the world that he gave his one and only Son, that whoever believes in him shall not perish but have eternal life" (John 3:16).

Posting up is related to rebounds. If the first-quarter game plan calls for the big guys or gals to post up, do it well! Get them the ball where they like it. Play to each other's strengths. Trust each other. He or she will kick the ball back out if there's no shot there. So much about basketball and life is about trust. It's the same with God. Take out another American dollar bill. American currency says, "In God we trust." You need to ask yourself, "Is that true for me?" How can trusting in God help? How does trusting in my coaches and teammates help?

Well, if we trust in God and His good plan for our lives, we won't fret about how many minutes we play today. We'll rejoice in the fact that we are players and that we can play this game we love. Trust can help us keep our composure when emotions run high. We won't argue with the refs. We won't trash talk, and we'll rebuke any trash talk directed at us. We'll express our joy without being cocky and obnoxious.

"Trust in the Lord with all your heart and lean not on your own understanding: in all your ways submit to him, and he will make your paths straight" (Proverbs 3:5).

I watched Stephen Curry explode for seventeen points in overtime to beat my Portland Trail Blazers last night. It was one of the most incredible displays in the history of the NBA. Right after the game, a sportscaster approached Curry, and he began the interview by saying, "All glory to God!" That's true. I just wish it didn't happen while playing the Trail Blazers!

SECOND QUARTER—ADJUSTMENTS

Almost every plan needs some adjustment. Some adjustments are large. Some are minor. Adjustments are important. The team that makes good adjustments has a serious competitive edge. Most second-quarter adjustments are small. We can make larger adjustments at halftime. No matter how small or how large, adjustments are important. They are vital to the team's success. They are also vital to your success.

God asks us to make adjustments all the time. Spend more time in His Word. Adjust your attitude toward Him, or your coach, a teacher, your parents, a brother, a sister, or a teammate.

What adjustments do you need to make right now? Be honest with yourself. Ask a close friend what adjustments they think you should make. Feedback is our friend.

_____

_____

_____

_____

_____

_____

_____

_____

If some adjustments seem too big to handle alone, remember, *you can always ask for help.*

Asking for help is not a sign of weakness but of strength! In basketball, asking for help is a sign of being coachable. Coaches love to work with coachable kids. I like to think of coaching like a feedback loop. You know how cool it is when you and your teammates are running a really good weave? It's giving and receiving. When the weave is running smoothly, it creates flow. Communication flow. Physical flow. Energy flow. A lot of offense is built around the weave.

You've just identified the adjustments you need to make. Now, allow me to ask you this: How flexible are you? How willing are you to adjust to things people ask of you? I recently read a story about a young college player who was a superstar in high school. He was early in his sophomore year in college, and his coach wasn't giving him many minutes. The coach was frustrated with his player's shot selection and lack of intensity in other areas of the game.

It took a month of sulking before the player decided to adjust. He

then refocused his game on the directions of his coach. The directions went something like this: "Pass first and play intensely on defense. Your offense will come from this adjustment to your game." It took about three games before he saw the true wisdom of his coach's plea. With a pass-first mentality and intense lockdown defense, not only did he begin to shoot within the flow of the offense, he helped create the flow of the offense! Soon double-doubles became the norm, and, more importantly, the team's winning percentage climbed significantly. Words like *strong-willed, stubborn, independent, inconsistent,* and *weak follow-through* may be clues that let you know that, with God's help, it is time to make a change. Flexibility can be your friend.

Two scriptures come to mind:

"Cause me to hear Your lovingkindness in the morning, for in You do I trust; cause me to know the way in which I should walk, for I lift up my soul to You" (Psalm 143:8, NKJV).

"Therefore humble yourselves under the mighty hand of God, that He may exalt you in due time, casting all your care upon Him, for He cares for you" (1 Peter 5:6–7, NKJV).

"This is a humbling experience. I'm so grateful."

—Chris Paul in his first press conference
upon arriving to the LA Clippers

"Humility is the key," says Kevin Durant. Why? "Because the Bible says so."

Being humble helps with adjustments and being more flexible.

HALFTIME

Halftime is a time for your coaches to help the team make larger adjustments. You see, while you've been playing, your coach has been observing. Maybe he or she needs to see more energy and motivation from the team. Maybe the playbook will be pulled out and a different offense or defense will be reviewed. Possibly, you're playing well and the coach just wants you to rest and be encouraged. Maybe halftime will be a feedback loop. You hear from the coach, and he or she asks you what adjustments need to be made. Are you being out-hustled? Has your team been playing the other team's style of play, and now you need to get back to your style of play? Are you going to change your approach to playing defense? Have you been losing the battle in the paint? Whatever is called for, be attentive. That's right; pay attention!

If coach asks for more energy, then give more energy. If you need to talk more to each other on the floor, then talk more. Don't just talk.

Communicate. Talk with a purpose. Fire each other up. Point out what's happening on the floor. Encourage each other.

There is nothing worse than getting brought down by the criticism of your own teammate. Lift each other up!

I remember a halftime break as a coach when we were basically getting beat by an outstanding shooting guard who was a sharpshooter and great at getting to the rim. We had never seen a player in our league this good. We had also never double-teamed a player. Our halftime strategy was to double-team him. This called for excellent communication from our remaining three players. It was fun to watch. Everyone was moving and talking on defense. Their sharpshooter got frustrated. We climbed back into the game and won a thriller. It was nothing but excitement for the players after the game!

THIRD QUARTER—ENERGY

I've always been fascinated by the third quarter of a game. If you are only playing with a timed half, I'm referring to the first half of the second half of the game. Adjustments at halftime have been made. There is not quite the intensity of the final quarter or final half of the game. Yet it is an important time. I think of this time as energy and execution time. Let's unpack these two.

ENERGY: The team that comes out of the halftime break with the most energy is often the team that wins. At its simplest level, the team that is building momentum, that has the opposing team playing their game, that is getting the most rebounds, that steals, that uses "energy" plays, is setting themselves up for success.

So, my question here for you is do you know how your approach to the third quarter or second half is affecting the game? Another way to think about it is to ask yourself, "Am I up for doing whatever it takes to win this game?" Energy is contagious. If your teammates need a spark, can the spark be you? Sometimes the coach creates a spark. It can come from the crowd. The crowd is often the reason teams win more games at home than on the road. Energy matters. Think about that.

Jesus was more than a spark. He is the Way, the Truth, and the Life! Demons tremble and flee in the name of Jesus. Jesus brought a young girl and an old man named Lazarus back from the dead! Imagine what that sparked in the hearts of His disciples! Now imagine what was felt by Lazarus's sisters. I'm imagining it takes a lot of energy to raise someone from the dead.

Only God can do such things. All we are doing is giving our best to win a basketball game. The energy you bring is important. Write down three ways you choose to bring out the positive energy you and your team need to build the momentum necessary to win the fourth quarter and the game:

1.

2.

3.

One last question I have for you is, "Are you in your best physical conditioning?" Are you giving your all in practice and pushing yourself in the weight room or in the gym? Chances are, if you have the physical stamina to create the type of energy we are talking about, you can be the spark your team may be looking for!

Nate Robinson was a sparkplug kind of player in college and in the NBA. He is a man of faith; look up some of his highlights. He could spark the entire gym to erupt with positive energy!

FOURTH QUARTER—EXECUTION

Your team may be up or down, or the score may be tied going into the fourth quarter or second part of the second half. No matter what the score, how well you execute is critically important to the end result. Everything we've been talking about comes into play now.

Are we passionate? Are we disciplined? Are we spirited and energetic? Are we following the coach's plan? Are we listening to the Holy Spirit and trusting what we hear and know to be true? Are we playing with Jesus above the rim?

Let me offer some favorite scriptures to remind us about passion, discipline, and the Holy Spirit.

Passion: "Be alert, stand firm in the faith, be brave and strong. Your every action must be done with love" (1 Corinthians 16:13–14, CSB).

Discipline: "Do you not know that the runners in a stadium all race, but only one receives the prize? Run in such a way that you may win. Now everyone who competes exercises self-control in everything" (1 Corinthians 9:24–25, CSB).

"Therefore I do not run like one who runs aimlessly, or box like one who beats the air. Instead, I discipline my body and bring it under strict control, so that after preaching to others, I myself will not be disqualified" (1 Corinthians 9: 26–27).Holman Christian Standard Bible

Holy Spirit: " For John baptized with water, but in a few days you will be baptized with the Holy Spirit. not many days from now . . . But you will receive power when the Holy Spirit has come upon you." (Acts 1:5 &8).NIV Life Application Study Bible

Imagine this. We are playing passionately, we are disciplined, and we are guided by the Holy Spirit who lives inside us. We are playing above the rim. Looks great, right?

Before Stephen Curry exploded for seventeen points in the Game 4 over-time win I mentioned earlier, he missed his first ten attempts at a three-point shot. Then he hit his first three-pointer and he did what he often does. He pounds his chest at the heart and then points one finger in the air to acknowledge and thank God. He and his mom made up that routine when he was in college. By the way, Stephen Curry was just awarded his second NBA MVP award today, and he is the first player to ever have the vote be unanimous. Everyone agreed!

Steph Curry

Please remember, Stephen Curry doesn't play basketball alone. What they did in Portland and how they won seventy-four games, one more than the record-breaking Chicago Bulls, required fourth-quarter execution. Picks, screens, rolls, stolen passes, rebounds, foul shots, and teamwork are on execution display. It just helps if you have a teammate like Stephen Curry!

What I have to say about all of this is that when we are playing with Jesus above the rim, we are winners regardless of the outcome of any individual game. Let that sink in. We are winners regardless of the outcome of any individual game! Do I want to win them all? Yes. Do I want to win a championship? Yes. Is there a higher prize to play for? Yes!

Are Stephen Curry and the Golden State Warriors going to win every game they play in the 2016–2017 season? No. Will they win the NBA championship? Maybe. Will Stephen Curry be any less a man of God if they don't win? No. Why? Because Stephen Curry plays with Jesus above the rim, and on this team he is not alone.

In 2003, when the Detroit Shock won the WNBA Championship, was Ruth Riley, who won the MVP award, happy? You bet she was! Did she remain humble and express gratitude for all that was accomplished? Yes. Why? Because Ruth Riley played her basketball career with Jesus above the rim!

Let's close with a look back at the trash talker. You probably will know little to nothing about what the trash talker has gone through in life. Whatever has motivated them to talk trash, your response may alter the course of their life. Maybe they've been abused. It's possible one or both of their parents has been missing in their lives.

They may be looking at the wrong role model, and they may think they have to talk trash in order to be successful.

Whatever the case may be, how we respond matters. It matters in our lives, and it may very well matter in their lives. What the trash talker is not expecting is to be met face-to-face with love. They are attempting to throw you off of your game, to intimidate you, and to cause you to doubt yourself and your team. They want to get under your skin. They want to frustrate you. Talking back only puts you in their space. Love, however, may freak them out and cause them to doubt.

Jesus talks about loving your enemies and turning the other cheek. Why? Because in doing so you are "heaping hot coals upon their head." The trash talker expects your anger. What does he or she think when you remain calm? What do they think if your response is love? What if you just keep smiling? They are then left alone to deal with their own behavior. Think about that. Jesus asks us to be a light in the darkness. He then goes further and asks us to step out, to not be a light hidden beneath the bed, but to be a light in the darkness hoisted onto a lamppost for all to see. We can't do this alone. "With man this is impossible, but with God all things are possible" (Matthew 19:26). NIV

When Jesus ascended to Heaven, He left us with His Holy Spirit. Passion, discipline, and the Holy Spirit.

Let's play with Jesus above the rim! I can't wait to see you there.

God bless you all, players, coaches, parents, refs, and fans alike. With Jesus, the game is never over!

Source: SPORTSSHEW

*L*et me add one final illustration.

Stephen (Curry) has teamed up with "Nothing But Nets", a campaign under the United Nation, that aims to stop a malaria epidemic that affects thousands of families in Africa.

Every 60 seconds, a child is killed by malaria. The organization provides mosquito nets treated with insecticide to save the lives of families in need in Sub-Saharan Africa.

Curry was more than happy to step up and not only help these families, but bring awareness to these staggering numbers. He thought the best way to do it was to incorporate it into his play on the court.

You won't believe what he agreed to and how many lives he has potentially saved because of it. He vowed that for every 3-pointer he makes, he would personally donate 3 mosquito nets to the foundation. In the first year he participated, the 2012-13 season, he broke the NBA record for 3-pointers in a season with 272 3-pointers.

He came close the next season with 261. Then he broke his own record in 2014-15 with 286. And last year, he shattered the record with 402 3-pointers.

Over the last 4 seasons, he has personally saved the lives of over 3,663 families. The Warriors have also joined his cause and match his donations every season. So the total comes to over 7, 326 families!

That's playing with Jesus, above the rim.

God bless you all, players, coaches, parents, refs and fans alike. With Jesus, the game is never over!

CPSIA information can be obtained
at www.ICGtesting.com
Printed in the USA
FSOW03n0644070217
30490FS